What is Mathematics?

SonLight Education Ministry
United States of America

D1710477

A Suggested Daily Schedule

(Adapt this schedule to your family needs.)

5:00 a.m.  Arise–Personal Worship

6:00 a.m. Family Worship and Bible Class–With Father

7:00 a.m. Breakfast

8:00 a.m. Practical Arts*–Domestic Activities
Agriculture
Industrial Arts
(especially those related to
the School Lessons)

10:00 a.m. School Lessons
(Take a break for some physical exercise
during this time slot.)

12:00 p.m. Dinner Preparations
(Health class could be included at this time
or a continued story.)

1:00 p.m. Dinner

2:00 p.m. Practical Arts* or Fine Arts
(Music and Crafts)
(especially those related to
the School Lessons)

5:00 p.m. Supper

6:00 p.m. Family Worship–Father
(Could do History Class)

7:00 p.m. Personal time with God–Bed Preparation

8:00 p.m. Bed

*Daily nature walk can be in morning or afternoon.

The Desire of All Nations

This book is a part of a curriculum that is built upon the life of Christ entitled, "The Desire of All Nations," for grades 2-8. Any of the books in this curriculum can be used by themselves or as an entire program.

INFORMATION ABOUT THE 2-8 GRADE PROGRAM

Multi-level

This program is written on a multi-level. That means that each booklet has material for grades 2-8. This is so the whole family in these grades may work from the same books. It is difficult for a busy mother to have 2 or more children and each have a different set of books. Remember, the Bible is written for all ages.

The Bible—the Primary Textbook

The books in this program are designed to teach the parent and the student how to learn academic subjects by using the Bible as a primary textbook.

The Desire of Ages

The Desire of Ages by Ellen G. White is used as a textbook to go with the Bible. This focuses on the early life of Christ, when He was a child. Children relate best to Christ as a child and youth.

Lesson Numbers

The big number in the top right corner on the cover of this book is the Lesson Number and corresponds with the chapter number in the book *The Desire of Ages*. For example, Lesson 1 in the school program will go along with chapter 1 in *The Desire of Ages*. Usually each family starts at the beginning with Lesson 1. Most children have not had a true Bible program, therefore they need the foundation built. If there is academic material that they have already covered, they do the Bible part and review then pass quickly on.

Seven Academic Subjects

There are seven academic subjects in this program—Health, Mathematics, Music, Science–Nature, History/Geography/Prophecy, Language, Voice–Speech.

Language Program

A good, solid language program is recommended to be used along with the SonLight materials.

The Riggs Institute has a multi-sensory teaching method that accommodates every child's unique learning style. Their program is called *Writing and Spelling Road to Reading and Thinking*. Order by calling (800) 200-4840 or visit www.riggsinst.org. (Disclaimer: SonLight does not endorse the reading books recommended in the Riggs' program.)

Another option which you might find more user friendly and is similar to the Riggs program but from a Christian perspective is *Spell to Write and Read* by Wanda Sanseri. To order, call Wanda Sanseri at (503) 654-2300 or visit https://www.bhibooks.net/swr.html

"God With Us"
Lesson 1 – Love

The following books are those you will need for this lesson.
All of these can be obtained from www.sonlighteducation.com

The Rainbow Covenant – Study the spiritual meaning of colors and make your own rainbow book.

Health
What is Health?

Math
What is Mathematics?

Music
What is Music?

Science/Nature
What is Nature?

A Casket – Coloring book and story. Learn how to treat the gems of the Bible.

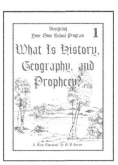

H/G/P
What is History, Geography and Prophecy?

Language
What is Language?

Speech/Voice
What is the Voice?

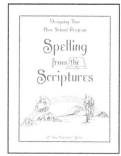

Spelling from the Scriptures

Bible Study – Learn how to study the Bible and helpful use tools.

Bible
The Desire of all Nations I
Teacher Study Guide

Student Study Guide

Bible Lesson Study Guide

Memory Verses
The Desire of all Nations I
Scripture Songs Book

and MP3 files

Our Nature Study Book – Your personal nature journal.

Outline of "The Desire of all Nations" Lesson 1

Bible	Health	Math	Music	Nature	H/G/P	Language	Voice
Week 1 **Month 1**							
Lesson 1							
Day 1							Language and Voice = How God's royal people should write, speak, and act to prepare for His kingdom.
Family Morning Worship *Covenant Notebook* (1) Music, Prayer, MV (2) Read pages 1-2 in the "Covenant Notebook" and discuss. (3) Sometime during the day take a nature walk looking for rainbows. (4) Begin finding pictures of complete rainbows to put into the plastic sheets behind the "Rainbows" page. Read and discuss the "Rainbows" page.	Use these songs during this week. "All Things Bright & Beautiful," "This is My Father's World," and "We Shall Know." Find this music in *Christ in Song* book which is included in these materials under the title "Song Books."						

READ THIS BEFORE BEGINNING

Cover the Teacher's Section of each school book before beginning that subject.
It is best to cover only a few concepts at once and understand them well and not run a marathon with a young person's mind. If this outline moves to fast for you SLOW down. Teach one idea and teach it well!

This school program is not a race with time, rather it is an experience with God.
The parents are to represent their Father in Heaven before the children—students.
Together learn about the Character Qualities and help one another in a godly manner to reach the finish line together.

INSTRUCTIONS

Bible	Health	Math	Music	Nature	H/G/P	Language	Voice
Day 2 (1) Music, Prayer, MV (2) Read page 3 in the "Covenant Notebook" and discuss. (Also use page 7)	Lay out Lesson 1 of the School Program showing the the front covers of each book, *What is Health?, What is Mathematics?, What is Music?, What is Nature?,*	*What is H/G/P?, What is Language?, and What is Voice?.* Each book will have a color cover of one of the colors of the rainbow. Place them in order as the rainbow colors	deomonstrate in a picture. Refer to page 7 of the *Covenant Notebook* to see what each color means and how it relates to the subject that bears that color.	(Examples: Health = Christ sacrificed His body on the cross for you. Mathematics = Deals in numbers saved and lost.	Music = Right music can turn our thoughts from things of this world to Divinity. Nature = Right growth in character.	H/G/P = The history of obedience and disobedience; geography of lands where the gospel is to be spread; prophecy telling us the future of those keeping the law.	

Bible	Health	Math	Music	Nature	H/G/P	Language	Voice

(3) Sometime during the day take a nature walk looking for rainbows.

(4) Begin finding pictures of complete rainbows to put into the plastic sheets behind the "Rainbows" page. Read and discuss the "Rainbows" page.

Day 3-4

(1) Music, Prayer, MV

(2) Read pages 4-9 in the "Covenant Notebook" and discuss.

(3) Sometime during the day take a nature walk looking for white items (or the color pages).

(4) Begin finding pictures of white things in nature to put into the plastic sheets behind the "White" page. Read and discuss the "White" page.

Day 5

Review what you have learned.

INSTRUCTIONS

Once the white page is completed then move on to the red page and so forth, always finding things from nature for your pictures. And on your nature walks fine the color you are currently working on. Do not look for man made things! Before going on the nature walk each day, read and discuss the information in the color section.

After day 5, and reviewing only what you have learned to that point, plan only to work on the *Covenant Notebook* one day a week until that book is finished (Use time in the afternoon and not during the regular school hours). However, do not forget to review the *Covenant Notebook* when you deem it necessary, and if you should find a new picture for it, stop and put it into *Covenant Notebook*. It gives you an opportunity to review lessons with the children.

Lesson 12 of Nature in this series is about the rainbow and would be a wonderful time to make a recommitment to God.

This *Covenant Notebook* is to prepare you for the 2-8 School Lessons. On week 2 begin the School Lessons.

Bible	Health	Math	Music	Nature	H/G/P	Language	Voice
Week 2 Lesson 1		START THE 2-8 PROGRAM, "The Desire Of All Nations."					
Day 1 "God With Us" (1) Music ("O Come, O come, Immanuel," "I Love Thee," "Thou didst Leave Thy Throne"), Prayer, MV (Mt 1:21) (2) Read and discuss Ge 3:14-15; 12:1-3. Discuss the Character Quality.	**Day 1** *What Is Health?* (1) Open Bibles and read II Sa 20:9. (2) Read or tell information. Do pages 1-17 or what you can cover. Discuss.	**Day 1** *What Is Math...?* (1) Open Bibles and read Mt 11:29. (2) Read or tell information. Do pages 1-8 or what you can cover. Discuss.				**Day 1** *Writing and Spelling Road to Reading and Thinking (WSRRT)* (1) Do your daily assignments for *WSRRT*. If you are still working on this program continue until you finish at least the 2nd teacher's notebook.	

INSTRUCTIONS

If you are still using the *Family Bible Lessons* do them for one of your worships each day and use *The Desire of all Nations* for the other worship each day.

These are the items you will need for worship for *The Desire of all Nations* Bible program: Old King James Bible (**NOT** the New King James Bible)

"*The Desire of all Nations*," Volume 1. Study Guide for the KJV Bible Lessons

The Desire of all Nations Teacher and Student Study Guides #1 (Chapters from *The Desire of Ages* Bible text book)

The Desire of all Nations Song Book #1 and CD Music #1 for Memory Verses

Christ in Song Song Book #1, 2, 3, 4

These are the items you will need for class time:

What is Health?; What is Mathematics?; What is Music?; What is Nature?; What is H/G/P?; What is Language?; and What is Voice?.

Our Nature Study Book "The Casket" Story & Coloring Book

Bible Study

Road Map and Route Catalogue

Bible	Health	Math	Music	Nature	H/G/P	Language	Voice
Day 2 "God With Us" (1) Music ("O Come, O come, O come, Immanuel," "I Love Thee," "Thou didst Leave Thy Throne"), Prayer, MV (Mt 1:21; Jn 8:28) (2) Read and discuss Gal 3:16; Ge 18:17-19; II Sam 7:12-17.	**Day 2** *What Is Health?* (1) Open Bibles and read I Co 12:23. (2) Read or tell information. Do pages 18-26 or what you can cover. Discuss.	**Day 2** *What Is Math...?* (1) Open Bibles and read Luke 6:38; Is 40:12; Ps 147:4; Is 40:26; Job 28:25. (2) Read or tell information. Do pages 9-22 or what you can cover. Discuss. **END**				**Day 2** *Writing and Spelling Road to Reading and Thinking* (1) Do your daily assignments for *WSRRT*.	
Day 3 "God With Us" (1) Music, Prayer, MV (Mt 1:21; Jn 8:28) (2) Read and discuss Ez 21:25-27; Lu 1:32; Isa 9:6-7.	**Day 3** *What Is Health?* (1) Open Bibles and read Pr 26:2. (2) Read or tell information. Do pages 27-35 or what you can cover. Discuss.		**Day 3** *What Is Music?* (1) Open Bibles and read Zeph 3:17. (2) Read or tell information. Do pages 1-6 or what you can cover. Discuss.			**Day 3** *Writing and Spelling Road to Reading and Thinking* (1) Do your daily assignments for *WSRRT*.	
Day 4 "God With Us" (1) Review what you have already covered.	**Day 4** *What Is Health?* (1) Review pages 1-35.	**Day 4** *What Is Math...?* (1) Review.	**Day 4** *What Is Music?* (1) Open Bibles and read Re 14:2-3. (2) Read or tell information. Do pages 7-17 or what you can cover. Discuss.			**Day 4** *Writing and Spelling Road to Reading and Thinking* (1) Do your daily assignments for *WSRRT*.	
Day 5	**Day 5**	**Day 5**	**Day 5**			**Day 5** Review	

Find practical applications from your textbooks you have thus far used this week. You will find them listed under **"Reinforce."** Choose and use today.

Bible	Health	Math	Music	Nature	H/G/P	Language	Voice
Week 3 **Lesson 1** **Day 1** "God With Us" (1) Music, Prayer, MV (Mt 1:21; Jn 8:28) (2) Read and discuss Ps 45:1-8; 72:1-11; Is 53.	**Day 1** *What Is Health?* (1) Open Bibles and read James 5:14. (2) Read or tell information. Do pages 36-39 or what you can cover. Discuss.		**Day 1** *What Is Music?* (1) Open Bibles and read I Ki 19:12. (2) Read or tell information. Do pages 18-30 or what you can cover. Discuss.			**Day 1** *Writing and Spelling Road to Reading and Thinking* (1) Do your daily assignments for *WSRRT.*	
Day 2 "God With Us" (1) Music, Prayer, MV (Mt 1:21; Jn 8:28; Jn 8:50) (2) Read and discuss Zec 12:10; Jn 14:9; Mt 1:23; Jn 1:1-4.	**Day 2** *What Is Health?* (1) Open Bibles and read De 34:7. (2) Read or tell information. Do pages 40-44 or what you can cover. Discuss.		**Day 2** *What Is Music?* (1) Open Bibles and read I Chr 13:8. (2) Read or tell information. Do pages 31-52 or what you can cover. Discuss. END			**Day 2** *Writing and Spelling Road to Reading and Thinking* (1) Do your daily assignments for *WSRRT.*	
Day 3 "God With Us" (1) Music, Prayer, MV (Mt 1:21; Jn 8:28; Jn 8:50; Phil 2:5-11) (2) Read and discuss *The Desire of Ages* 19-20:0.	**Day 3** *What Is Health?* (1) Open Bibles and read Ez 33:11. (2) Read or tell information. Do pages 45-53 or what you can cover. Discuss.			**Day 3** *What Is Nature?* (1) Open Bibles and read Ro 13:10. (2) Read or tell information. Do pages 1-11 or what you can cover. Discuss.		**Day 3** *Writing and Spelling Road to Reading and Thinking* (1) Do your daily assignments for *WSRRT.*	

Bible	Health	Math	Music	Nature	H/G/P	Language	Voice
Day 4 "God With Us" (1) Music, Prayer, MV (Mt 1:21; Jn 8:28; Jn 8:50; Phil 2:5-11) (2) Read and discuss *The Desire of Ages* 20:2-21:0.	**Day 4** *What Is Health?* (1) Open Bibles and read De 7:15; De 32:46; and Pr 4:20, 22. (2) Read or tell information. Do pages 54-60 or what you can cover. Discuss.			**Day 4** *What Is Nature?* (1) Open Bibles and read Ps 40:5; Ps 111:4. (2) Read or tell information. Do pages 12-17 or what you can cover. Discuss.		**Day 4** *Writing and Spelling Road to Reading and Thinking* (1) Do your daily assignments for *WSRRT*.	
Day 5 "God With Us" (1) Review.	**Day 5** *What Is Health?* (1) Review pages 1-60.	**Day 5** *What Is Math....?* (1) Review.	**Day 5** *What Is Music?* (1) Review.	**Day 5** *What Is Nature?* (1) Review pages 1-17.		**Day 5** *Writing and Spelling Road to Reading and Thinking* (1) Do your daily assignments for *WSRRT*.	
Week 4 Lesson 1 **Day 1** "God With Us" (1) Music, Prayer, MV (Mt 1:21; Jn 8:28; Jn 8:50; Phil 2:5-11) (2) Read and discuss *The Desire of Ages* 21:1-2.	**Day 1** *What Is Health?* (1) Open Bibles and read De 7:15; De 32:46; and Pr 4:20, 22. (2) Read the story. Do pages 61-80. Discuss.			**Day 1** *What Is Nature?* (1) Open Bibles and read Job 12:7-8. (2) Read or tell information. Do pages 18-23 or what you can cover. Discuss.		**Day 1** *Writing and Spelling Road to Reading and Thinking* (1) Do your daily assignments for *WSRRT*.	
Day 2 "God With Us" (1) Music, Prayer, MV (Mt 1:21; Jn 8:28; Jn 8:50; Phil 2:5-11) (2) Read and discuss *The Desire of Ages* 21:3-22:1.	**Day 2** *What Is Health* (1) Open Bibles and review De 7:15; De 32:46; and Pr 4:20, 22. (2) Do pages 81-86. Discuss. **END**			**Day 2** *What Is Nature?* (1) Open Bibles and read Ps 143:5. (2) Read or tell information. Do pages 24-30 or what you can cover. **END**		**Day 2** *WSRRT* (1) Do your daily assignments for *WSRRT*. Continue the *WSRRT* but add the Language lessons in whenever it is time to do them. **This will not be repeated.**	

Bible	Health	Math	Music	Nature	H/G/P	Language	Voice
Day 3 "God With Us" (1) Music, Prayer, MV (Mt 1:21; Jn 8:28; Jn 8:50; Phil 2:5-11) (2) Read and discuss *The Desire of Ages* 21:3-22:3.					**Day 3** *What Is H/G/P?* (1) Open Bibles and read He 1:10. (2) Read or tell information. Do pages 1-6 or what you can cover. Discuss. Choose a good mission book to begin reading as a family.	**Day 3** *What Is Language?* (1) Open Bibles and read Col 3:16. (2) Read or tell information. Do pages 1-10 or what you can cover + *WSRRT*. Discuss.	
Day 4 "God With Us" (1) Music, Prayer, MV (Mt 1:21; Jn 8:28; Jn 8:50; Phil 2:5-11) (2) Read and discuss *The Desire of Ages* 21:3-22:3.					**Day 4** *What Is H/G/P?* (1) Open Bibles and read Ps 119:105 & He 13:1. (2) Read or tell information. Do pages 7-14. Discuss.	**Day 4** *What Is Language?* (1) Open Bibles and read Pr 25:11. (2) Read or tell information. Do pages 11-17 + *WSRRT*. Discuss.	**Day 4** *What Is Voice?* (1) Open Bibles and read Ps 105:2. (2) Read or tell information. Do pages 1-4 Discuss.
Day 5 "God With Us" (1) Music, Prayer. (2) Read and discuss *The Desire of Ages* 22:4-24:1.	**Day 5** *What Is Health?* (1) Review	**Day 5** *What Is Math...?* (1) Review.	**Day 5** *What Is Music?* (1) Review.	**Day 5** *What Is Nature?* (1) Review.	**Day 5** *What Is H/G/P?* (1) Review pages 1-14.	**Day 5** *What Is Language?* (1) Review pages 1-17.	**Day 5** *What Is Voice?* (1) Review pages 1-4.
Week 1 (5) |Month 2| **Lesson 1** **Day 1** "God With Us" (1) Music, Prayer, MV. (2) Read and discuss *The Desire of Ages* 24:2-26:3.		If there is any information that the student should know and does not—REVIEW.			**Day 1** *What Is H/G/P?* (1) Open Bibles and read Jer 10:12. (2) Read or tell information. Do pages 15-25Aa or what you can cover. Discuss.	Do your daily assignments for *WSRRT*. **Day 1** *What Is Language?* (1) Open Bibles and read Jn 1:1. (2) Read or tell information. Do pages 18-22 or what you can cover. Discuss. **END**	**Day 1** *What Is Voice?* (1) Open Bibles and read Ps 32:2. (2) Read or tell information. Do pages 5-8. Discuss. **END**

Bible	Health	Math	Music	Nature	H/G/P	Language	Voice
Day 2 "God With Us" (1) Music, Prayer, MV. (2) Expand or review any part of the lesson. (Could use section about William Miller in H/G/P.)					**Day 2** *What Is H/G/P?* (1) Open Bibles and read II Pe 1:21. (2) Read or tell information. Do pages 26-47 or what you can cover. Discuss. (Story about "William Miller" may take longer.)	**Day 2** *Writing and Spelling Road to Reading and Thinking* (1) Do your daily assignments for *WSRRT*.	**Day 2** *What Is Voice?* (1) Review
Day 3 "God With Us" (1) Music, Prayer, MV. (2) Expand or review any part of the lesson. (Could use the section in H/G/P. "The Schools of the Prophets.")					**Day 3** *What Is H/G/P?* (1) Open Bibles and read Ja 3:17 & Pr 9:10. (2) Read or tell information. Do pages 48-65 or what you can cover. Discuss.	**Day 3** *Writing and Spelling Road to Reading and Thinking* (1) Do your daily assignments for *WSRRT*.	
Day 4 "God With Us" (1) Music, Prayer, MV. (2) Expand or review any part of the lesson. (Could explain why the Apocrypha books are not included in Bible.) **END**					**Day 4** *What Is H/G/P?* (1) Open Bibles and read Ex 17:14 & Ge 5:22. (2) Read or tell information. Do pages 66-78 or what you can cover. Discuss. **END**	**Day 4** *Writing and Spelling Road to Reading and Thinking* (1) Do your daily assignments for *WSRRT*.	**Day 4-5** Use this time to review anything from lesson 1.

On day 5 review any subject in Lesson 1 that needs a better understanding.

Continue the process with Lesson 2. See the *Road Map and Route Catalogue.*

Week 2 | **Month 2**

Lesson 2

Day 1

"The Chosen People" (1) Music, Prayer, MV. (2) Read and discuss.

Mathematics
Instructions

1. Try to make mathematics more concrete and enjoyable by making story problems from your Bible lesson and nature lesson; use a blackboard and write a problem out (or a stick writing in the dirt), letting the student work out the answer, then let the child give the teacher a problem; or, as you are working at a project, make it into a mathematics problem, etc. Help the student to see that mathematics is a simple part of life.

2. Practice mental problems— where the child has to work out the answer in his head.

3. Let the child work in whatever level he is capable of doing in the workbooks.

Table of Contents

$+$ $-$ X $\div$

Behold Christ

After the celebrated painter Da Vinci had completed his immortal painting of the "Last Supper," a friend came in to inspect it. "That goblet is wonderful," said the friend; "it stands out like solid silver." The devout artist dashed his brush over the goblet in an instant and exclaimed, "Nothing shall draw the eye of the beholder from my Lord!" O Christian worker, keep Christ in the foreground. Let nothing hide thy Saviour from the sight of men. Your mission is to point out "...*Behold the Lamb of God, which taketh away the sin of the world*" (John 1:29).

Teacher Section

"Learn of me; for I am meek and lowly in heart...."

Matthew 11:29

Step 1

Study the Bible Lesson and begin to memorize the Memory Verses. Familiarize Yourself With the Character Quality. The student can answer the Bible Review Questions. See page 6. Use the Steps in Bible Study.

Bible Lesson

"God With Us" – Genesis 3:14-15; 12:1-3; Galatians 3:16; Genesis 49:10; Deuteronomy 18:17-19; II Samuel 7:12-17; Ezekiel 21:25-27; Luke 1:32; Isaiah 9:6-7; Psalm 45:1-8; 72:1-11; Isaiah 53; Zechariah 12:10; John 14:9; Matthew 1:23; John 1:1-4

Memory Verses

Matthew 1:23; 1:20-21; John 8:28; 6:57; 7:18; 8:50; Philippians 2:5-11

Character Quality

Love – an affection of the mind excited by beauty and worth of any kind, or by the qualities of an object; charity or **love**.

Antonyms – hate; detestableness; abomination; loathing; scorn; disdainfulness; selfishness

Character Quality Verse

I Corinthians 13:4-7 – *"Charity [love] suffereth long, and is kind; charity envieth not; charity vaunteth not itself, is not puffed up,*

"Doth not behave itself unseemly, seeketh not her own, is not easily provoked, thinketh no evil;

"Rejoiceth not in iniquity, but rejoiceth in the truth;

"Beareth all things, believeth all things, hopeth all things, endureth all things."

Step 2

Understand How To/ And

A. Do the Spelling Cards so the student can begin to build his own spiritual dictionary.

B. Mark Your Bible.

C. Evaluate Your Student's Character in relation to the character quality of **love**.

D. Familiarize Yourself With "What is Mathematics?" Notice the Projects.

E. Review the References for "Mathematics."

F. Notice the Answer Key.

A. Spelling Cards
Spelling Lists

Math Words	Emmanuel
Place I - II - III	enmity
addition	forever
algebra	head
decimal	heel
division	Judah
fraction	kingdom
geometry	lawgiver
inclined	**love**
learn	peace
mathematics	Prophet
multiplication	sceptre (or er)
subtraction	seed
	Shiloh
Bible Words	throne
blessing	woman
bruise	

Place I = Grades 2-3-4
Place II = Grades 4-5-6
Place III = Grades 6-7-8

B. How to Mark the Bible

1. Copy the list of Bible texts in the back of the Bible on an empty page as a guide.

2. Go to the first text in the Bible and copy the next text beside it. Go to the next one and repeat the process until they are all chain referenced.

3. Have the student present the study to family and/or friends.

4. In each student lesson there is often one or more sections that have a Bible marking study on the subject studied. (See the student's section, pages 21-22.)

C. Evaluate Your Student's Character

This section is for the purpose of helping the teacher know how to encourage the students in becoming more **loving**. See page 7.

See the book
Spelling from the Scriptures
for instructions
about the Spelling Cards.

D. Familiarize Yourself With "What is Mathematics?" – Notice the Projects

Projects

1. What are the laws of **love** in your home? Make a list. Can you think of a new one your family may need. Practice it, and especially this week. (Example: All family members will be respectful of other peoples' things because they **love** them.)

2. Do you see mathematics in nature? Find examples on at least two days during your nature walks this week. Use your backpack. (Example: leaf pattern on a branch—spiral, alternating, parallel). Write the examples you find in *Our Nature Study Book*. Make a parallel to your Bible story and use the character quality of **love**.

Use three examples (1) numbers, (2) quantities, and (3) measurements.

3. Help the child think about Mathematics as he goes about his daily life. (Examples: the time he eats each day, the number of people eating at each meal, etc.) Have the child draw pictures of three laws of mathematics he experiences in his day (as relates to **love** and the Bible lesson).

4. Together, as a family, save enough money to purchase the book *Number in Scripture* by Bullinger to add to the family's library for a resource.

5. Do a survey with adults and ask them the question, "What is Mathematics?" Write down their answers. What did you learn from them?

Notes

E. Review the References for "Mathematics"

Teacher, read through this section before working on the lesson with the student.

See the student section, pages 21-22.

F. Notice the Answer Key

The answer key for the student section is found on page 8.

Step 3

Read the Lesson Aim.

Lesson Aim

This lesson is an introduction to mathematics. Teach your child the character quality of **love** through "God With Us" and *"What Is Mathematics?"*

"Satan represents God's law of **love** as a law of selfishness. He declares that it is impossible for us to obey its precepts. The fall of our first parents, with all the woe that has resulted, he charges upon the Creator, leading men to look upon God as the author of sin, and suffering, and death. Jesus was to unveil this deception. As one of us He was to give an example of obedience. For this He took upon Himself our nature, and passed through our experiences. *'In all things it behooved him to be made like unto his brethren'* (Hebrews 2:17). If we had to bear anything which Jesus did not endure, then upon this point Satan would represent the power of God as insufficient for us. Therefore Jesus was *'in all points tempted like as we are'* (Hebrews 4:15). He endured every trial to which we are subject. And He exercised in His own behalf no power that is not freely offered to us. As man, He met temptation, and overcame in the strength given Him from God. He says, *'I delight to do thy will, O my God: yea, thy law is within my heart'* (Psalm 40:8). As He went about doing good, and healing all who were afflicted by Satan, He made plain to men the character of God's law and the nature of His service. His life testifies that it is possible for us also to obey the law of God."*

Mathematics is based on law and it helps us to explain numbers, quantities, measurements, and the relations between them. As Jesus explained the law of **love** by coming to

*The Desire of Ages 24

this Earth, so does mathematics help explain the physical world we live in by the laws that govern it.

Mathematics also helps us demonstrate how the laws of numbers work in our everyday life. And, they can remind us how the character quality **love** would work practically in the life.

Step 4

Prepare to begin the Mathematics Lesson.

To Begin the Mathematics Lesson

Go for a mathematics walk and teacher can point out things in the home and outside in nature that relate to mathematics.

Step 5

Begin the Mathematics lesson. Cover only what can be understood by your student. Make the lessons a family project by all being involved in part or all of the lesson. These lessons are designed for the whole family.

Steps in Bible Study

1. Prayer

2. Read the verses/meditate/memorize.

3. Look up key words in *Strong's Concordance* and find their meaning in the Hebrew or Greek dictionary in the back of that book.

4. Cross reference (marginal reference) with other Bible texts. An excellent study tool is *The Treasury of Scripture Knowledge.*

5. Use Bible custom books for more information on the times.

6. Write a summary of what you have learned from those verses.

7. Mark key thoughts in the margin of your Bible.

8. Share your study with others to reinforce the lessons you have learned.

Review Questions

1. What were the circumstances under which the first promise of a Redeemer was given? (Genesis 3:14-15)

2. What promise was made to Abraham, and what did it mean? (Genesis 12:1-3; Galatians 3:16)

3. Through what tribe of Israel was the Messiah to come? (Genesis 49:10)

4. What promise was given through Moses? (Deuteronomy 18:17-19)

5. Through whom was the permanence of David's kingdom assured? (II Samuel 7:12-17; Ezekiel 21:25-27; Luke 1:32)

6. What exalted ideas concerning the Messiah were made prominent? (Isaiah 9:6, 7; Psalm 45:1-8; 72:1-11)

7. What also was foretold of His relation to sin? (Isaiah 53; Zechariah 12:10)

8. What is the significance of the name which John applies to Christ? (John 14:9; Matthew 1:23)

9. What important facts are stated of Him in John 1:1-4
    a.
    b.
    c.

10. As part of the great scheme of human redemption, what did the Word become? What is the meaning of the words *"became flesh?"* (Matthew 1:23)

Notes

Evaluating Your Child's Character

Check the appropriate box for your student's level of development,
or your own, as the case may be.

Maturing Nicely (MN), Needs Improvement (NI), Poorly Developed (PD), Absent (A)

Love

1. *"**Charity** suffereth long and is kind"* (I Corinthians 13:4). Does my child show a maturity of **love** that enables them to be kind while suffering from hunger, tiredness, or discomfort?

MN   NI   PD   A
❏   ❏   ❏   ❏

2. When the child encounters people with character deficiencies, is the child's reaction one of **loving** pity and concern instead of condemnation?

MN   NI   PD   A
❏   ❏   ❏   ❏

3. Does your child seem to **love** God more as a result of studying the material contained in the Bible?

MN   NI   PD   A
❏   ❏   ❏   ❏

4. *"**Charity**...vaunteth not itself; is not puffed up."* Does the child refrain from comparing himself with others? Do they make comments like "I can read better than _____ ."

MN   NI   PD   A
❏   ❏   ❏   ❏

5. *"**Charity**...seeketh not her own."* Is the child willing for others to have the best or the most of desirable things?

MN   NI   PD   A
❏   ❏   ❏   ❏

6. *"**Love** your enemies."* Does the child initiate reconciliation with or do kind things for those who have hard feelings toward him or who have treated him unfairly?

MN   NI   PD   A
❏   ❏   ❏   ❏

7. *"**Love** covers a multitude of sins."* Is the child eager to tell you about the failures of others or do they **lovingly** shield others from exposure where possible to do so with integrity?

MN   NI   PD   A
❏   ❏   ❏   ❏

8. *"**Charity**...thinketh no evil."* Is the child unsuspecting, ever placing the most favorable construction upon the motives and acts of others?

MN   NI   PD   A
❏   ❏   ❏   ❏

Page 5

Teacher, check.

Page 7

1. Learn

2. Character

3. God

Page 8

1. "Inclined to learn"

2. His character

3. Teacher, check.

4. Yes

5. Teacher, check.

6. Yes

7. **Love** of God

Mathematics

mat	mit	mat
he	me	that
ma	sit	tame
them	sat	cats
the	met	etc.

$$+ \quad - \quad x \quad \div$$
$$x = y$$

Page 13

A tree <u>adding</u> buds, blossoms, and fruit

An animal <u>subtracting</u> food from a tree to store for winter

A wasp <u>building</u> a nest

A tree <u>dividing</u> its leaves.

Page 15

Some examples:

1. John 14:3

2. Genesis 1 (each day new things added)

3. John 2:16

4. Matthew 14:15-20; Genesis 1:22

5. Genesis 1:4, 7, 14

Page 22

1. Using the laws God has made and working within these laws

2. See page 10.

3. See Matthew 13—the parables.

4. The garden

5. Prepares us to do good work

6. God

Gardening Sheet

Lesson _One_ **Subject** _Mathematics_

Title _"What is Mathematics?"_

In Season	Out of Season
Make a list of gardens or orchards as found in the Bible. See if you can glean any ideas from them to help you in planning your garden. Use scale paper to draw your garden plan. How can gardening teach you about the **love** of God and Mathematics (the laws He works with)?	Plan an indoor garden by building (using your mathematics) planter boxes. Plan where in the house you have south facing (most sunlight) windows. Which plants will be most usable to you for food in the winter?

Student
Section

"Who hath measured the waters in the hollow of his hand,
and meted out heaven with the span,
and comprehended the dust of the earth in a measure,
and weighed the mountains in scales,
and the hills in a balance?"
Isaiah 40:12

What Is Mathematics?

+
−
÷

Research

Introduction

"Learn of me; for I am meek and lowly in heart...."

Matthew 11:29

The word "mathematics" comes from a Greek word which means "inclined to learn." Learn what? Man says: learn the science and laws that explain numbers, quantities, measurements, and the relations between them. This is good to do, but God says, *"Learn of me; for I am meek and lowly in heart..."* (Matthew 11:29). So you see, it is not enough to just learn facts, we must also learn about God through those facts.

There are many types of studies in mathematics. **Arithmetic** is concerned with problems and numbers. **Algebra** works with solving equations where letters represent unknown quantities. **Geometry** teaches the properties and relationships of figures in space. As in mathematics, God wanted man to learn about

Mathematics =
"Inclined to Learn"

"Learn of Me"

$$4 + 3 = 7$$

$$4 - 1 = 3$$

$$2 \ x \ 5 \ = \ 10$$

$$24 \div 2 = 12$$

$3.50

$$\frac{1}{4}$$

$$A = 3y$$

$$C = 2$$

Addition • Subtraction • Multiplication •
Division • Fractions • Decimals •
Algebra • Geometry

His **love** so He sent His Son, Jesus, which is an example of that **love**. Each type of mathematics can teach us more about Him and His **love**.

Mathematics is important to help people in their practical, daily life. Some examples include simple tasks of telling time and counting our change at the store after a purchase. We can use mathematics for more complex tasks such as household accounting, figuring income tax, cooking, driving, gardening, and sewing. For people to live a practical, spiritual life each day they need an example. Jesus came to be that practical example. Mathematics can teach us how to live each day practically according to His ways and purposes.

Scientists use mathematics in astronomy, chemistry, and physics. Industry uses mathematics to design bridges, buildings, dams, highways, tunnels, and many other projects. In business, mathematics are used in buying and selling, in record keeping, calculating employees' hours and wages. Even our bodies work by numbers: the heart beats so many times a minute, the lungs have a certain capacity of air they can take in, there are a certain number of bones and muscles in the body. But, all of this knowledge is of no value if we do not have the character of God in our lives.

When adding up the deeds done this day what is the sum?

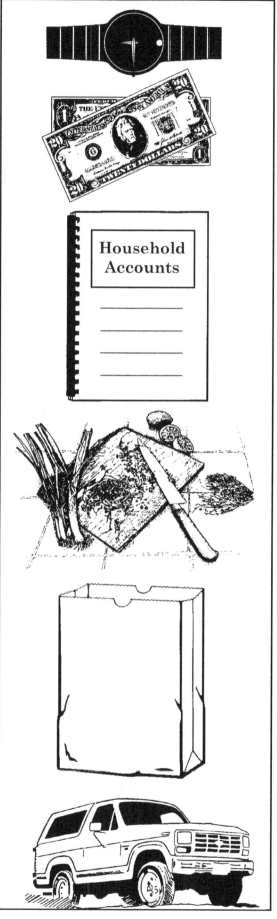

Household Accounts

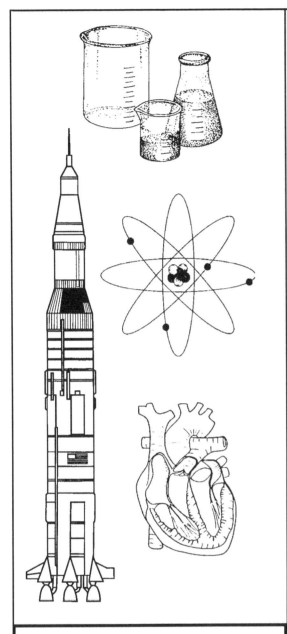

Jesus, in keeping within the laws of the human body, came in **love** as a baby!

" *'His name shall be called Immanuel,…God with us.' 'The light of the knowledge of the glory of God'* is seen *'in the face of Jesus Christ.'* From the days of eternity the Lord Jesus Christ was one with the Father; He was *'the image of God,'* the image of His greatness and majesty, *'the outshining of his glory.'* It was to manifest this glory that He came to our world. To this sin-darkened earth He came to reveal the light of God's **love** —to be *'God with us.'* Therefore it was prophesied of Him, *'His name shall be called Immanuel.'*

"By coming to dwell with us, Jesus was to reveal God both to men and to angels. He was the Word of God—God's thought made audible. In His prayer for His disciples He says, *'I have declared unto them thy name,'*—*'merciful and gracious, long-suffering, and abundant in goodness and truth,'*—*'that the* **love** *wherewith thou hast loved me may be in them,*

We Use Mathematics in Our Daily Lives.

How do you use mathematics when you sew?

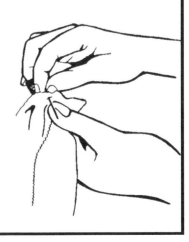

and I in them.' But not alone for His earthborn children was this revelation given. Our little world is the lesson book of the universe. God's wonderful purpose of grace, the mystery of redeeming **love**, is the theme into which *'angels desire to look,'* and it will be their study throughout endless ages. Both the redeemed and the unfallen beings will find in the cross of Christ their science and their song. It will be seen that the glory shining in the face of Jesus is the glory of self-sacrificing **love**. In the light from Calvary it will be seen that the law of self-renouncing **love** is the law of life for earth and heaven; that the **love** which *'seeketh not her own'* has its source in the heart of God; and that in the meek and lowly One is manifested the character of Him who dwelleth in the light which no man can approach unto."*

Reflect

Love

"...The law of self-renouncing **love** is the law of life for earth and heaven; that the **love** which seeketh not her own' has its source in the heart of God; and that in the meek and lowly One is manifested the character of Him..."

"Our little world is the lesson book of the universe."

"In the light from Calvary it will be seen that the law of self-renouncing **love** is the law of life for earth and heaven...."

"**Love** seeketh not her own."

*The Desire of Ages 19-20

Jesus Learned Mathematics In Nature And In The Carpenter's Shop

When Jesus was older He taught parables using Math. What was one of them?

An Example

"And the child grew, and waxed strong in spirit, filled with wisdom; and the grace of God was upon him."

Luke 2:40

As a child, Jesus lived within the laws of mankind. *"And the child grew, and waxed strong in spirit, filled with wisdom; and the grace of God was upon him."* He learned as children need to learn today. His mathematics study was taught through the practical duties of life. He learned mathematics through the things His own hands had in the beginning created in nature and the work he did in the carpenter's shop. As He recreated things of wood (from trees He had created) with mathematical calculations, so He would recreate men who would cooperate with Him.

Reflect

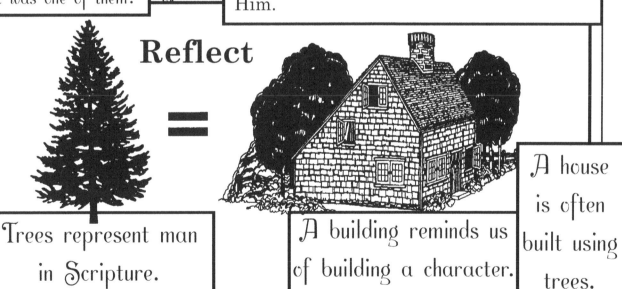

Trees represent man in Scripture.

A building reminds us of building a character.

A house is often built using trees.

Finish this statement by writing several sentences.
Jesus working in the carpenter's shop demonstrates how He builds character. He does this by_____.

Reflect
Mathematics/Law at Work

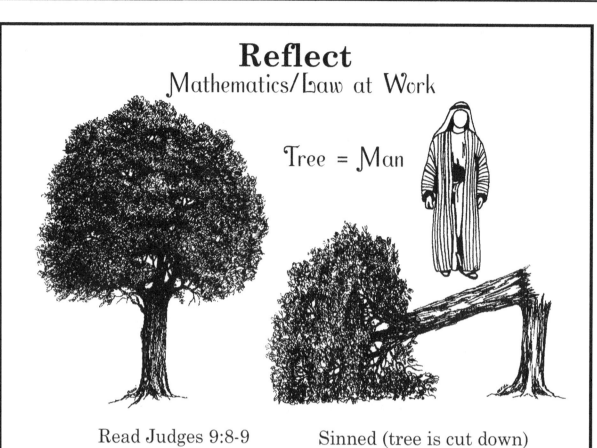

Tree = Man

Read Judges 9:8-9
and Psalm 1:3

Sinned (tree is cut down)

Jesus came into the carpenter
shop and recreated that piece
of dead wood into a beautiful
thing with a purpose. He did it by:

1. **Measuring** (need)
   (Revelation 11:1)

2. **Cutting** (trials)
   (7 *Testimonies* 264; I Peter 4:12)

3. **Building** (construction takes place)
   (Ephesians 2:21; Read *Messages
   to Young People* 15-18)

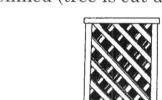

Review

Place I

1. Mathematics means "inclined to ___ ___ ___ ___ ___."

2. What can we learn about God? Ch ___ ___ ___ ___ ___ er

3. Mathematics teaches us about the character of ___ ___ ___ .

4. Read and color the picture below.

One special character quality of God is:

LOVE

Review
Place II - III

Answer these questions:

1. What does the word Mathematics mean?

2. What is man to learn about God?

3. Describe how Jesus recreates a man.

4. Can mathematics be a teacher of God's character?

5. Mathematics shows how laws work. Give an example.

6. Did Jesus follow the laws that govern our bodies when He lived on Earth?

7. What did Jesus come to reveal to people on this earth?

Reflect

From the word LOVE
we can make the word VOLE.
One meaning of this word is,
"to risk everything
in the hope of great profit."
Jesus risked everything in the
hope of redeeming you.

What other words can you make from the word Mathematics?

Examples: mat
Him (Jesus)

_____

_____

_____

_____

_____

_____

_____

_____

_____

_____

Give

Arnold, the celebrated chronometer maker, made the smallest watch ever seen in his day and presented it to George III, of England. It was so small that it was set as a jewel in a finger ring. It consisted of 120 parts, and weighed as many grains. The fly-wheel and pinion actually weighed only 1-17 part of a grain. The King was so pleased with the gift that he gave Arnold 500 guineas. The Emperor of Russia requested Arnold to make him a similar one, but he refused to do so, saying he wished his own sovereign to have such a watch as no one else should have in the whole world. In like manner, God has given you a unique gift in **love** for you, His own Son—Jesus.

Learning

Mathematics

The hand and the

soul working together

in **love!**

Research
Mind and Hand

"Give, and it shall be given unto you; good measure, pressed down, and shaken together, and running over...."
Luke 6:38

It is important to learn how to add and subtract. Ten dollars plus two must not stop there. What the mind needs to learn next must be how to put this to a practical use. For example, one could use the first dollar for an extra **love** offering to Jesus. Then, use the remaining money to buy a special **love gift** for Father's and Mother's anniversary. The gift may cost $10.00; so subtract the ten dollars from your eleven remaining dollars, giving you a total of one dollar left in your money box. This left over one dollar can be saved. Later, your grandparents send an unexpected gift of ten dollars which multiplies the amount you now have. So, after paying tithe and offering, the rest can go into your money box for saving and future use. God would have you use your money for unselfish purposes. (**How much do you have in your money box?**)

All of this is called practical, daily mathematics—using the laws God has made and working within these laws.

The Greek way of learning commits facts to memory in a classroom but usually does not apply them in a practical or spiritual way. It does not touch our daily lives or experience. An example is memorizing the multiplication or "times" tables but not using them that day or week in a practical way.

An example of applying your mathematics and using the times tables is to build a bird house by following these steps:

1. Draw a pattern
2. Figure what materials you will need
3. Buy the wood
4. Measure and mark out the pieces
5. Cut out the pieces
6. Find a spiritual lesson

Reflect – Nature

"Who hath measured the waters
in the hollow of his hand,
and meted out heaven
with the span,
and comprehended the dust
of the earth in a measure,
and weighed the mountains in scales,
and the hills in a balance?"

Isaiah 40:12

Reinforce

Read the story,
"The Lent
Half-Dollar"
on page 16.

Measured

Meted Out

Comprehended

Weighed

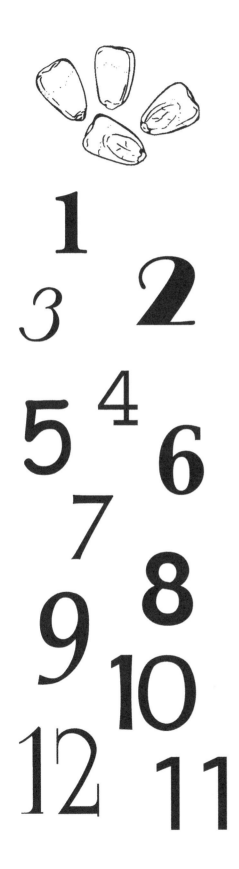

When you were young, you learned many things about mathematics through nature. You may not even have realized it. You might have helped your parents plant a row of corn and watched those seeds multiply into thousands of seeds. In this way you were learning mathematics. God wanted to teach you through this experience how His blessings multiply from small seeds of **love** planted here and there.

Bible

The Bible is full of numbers and the laws that govern them. Each letter, word, or sentence in the Bible was written at the right time in the right place, in the right order, and in the right number. God is the "Wonderful Numberer."

"He telleth the number of the stars; he calleth them all by their names" (Psalm 147:4). *"Lift up your eyes on high, and behold who hath created these things, that bringeth out their host by number: he calleth them all by names by the greatness of his might, for that he is strong in power; not one faileth"* (Isaiah 40:26). *"To make the weight for the winds; and he weigheth the waters by measure"* (Job 28:25).

Each number in the Bible has a particular meaning and in the next lessons we will learn more about those meanings. We will learn God's use of numbers to teach spiritual lessons rather than man's use of them.

Reinforce – Numbers and Their Meanings

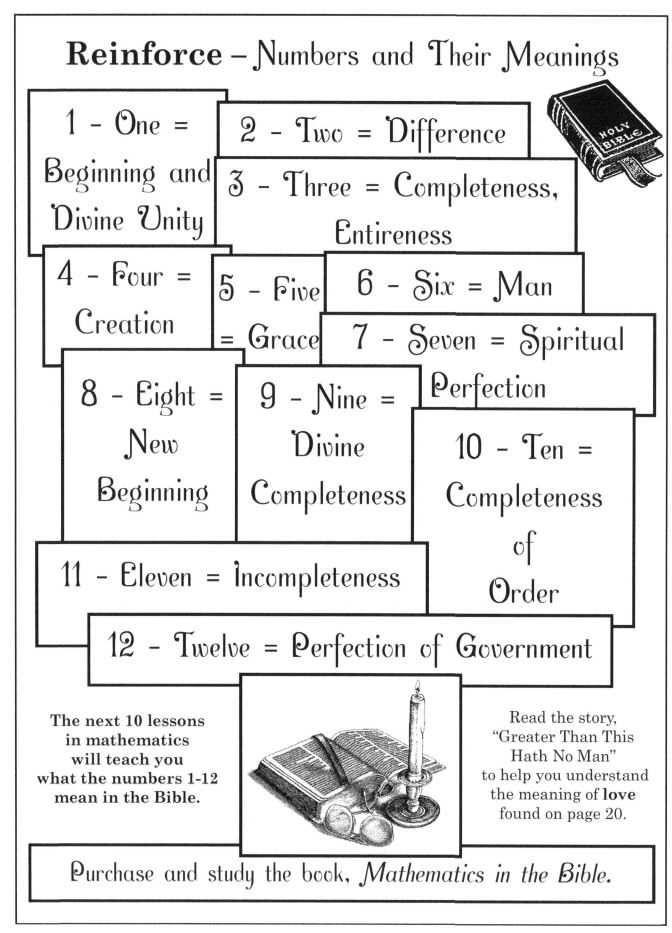

1 - One = Beginning and Divine Unity

2 - Two = Difference

3 - Three = Completeness, Entireness

4 - Four = Creation

5 - Five = Grace

6 - Six = Man

7 - Seven = Spiritual Perfection

8 - Eight = New Beginning

9 - Nine = Divine Completeness

10 - Ten = Completeness of Order

11 - Eleven = Incompleteness

12 - Twelve = Perfection of Government

The next 10 lessons in mathematics will teach you what the numbers 1-12 mean in the Bible.

Read the story, "Greater Than This Hath No Man" to help you understand the meaning of **love** found on page 20.

Purchase and study the book, *Mathematics in the Bible.*

Remind
Place I - II - III
Two Ways

1. GREEK
Mathematics

    A. Brain—Fact only
    B. Hands—Some practical

2. HEBREW
Mathematics

    A. Bible—Spiritual
    B. Brain—Facts
    C. Hands—Practical

Reinforce
Find an example of mathematics in nature.
Draw what you find below.

Where to Learn Mathematics

Have you noticed how Jesus almost always used an outdoor or country setting for most of His teachings when He lived on earth? In the very beginning He chose to have man till the soil which offered experience in using mathematics, such as:

(1) the increase of one seed to many,

(2) the size of space needed to plant,

(3) when to plant,

(4) calculating straight rows,

(5) the amount of space growing plants will need.

(6) to know what is the best way to use the produce of the garden in glorifying God.

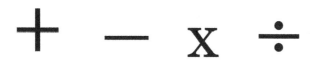

Object of Learning Mathematics

The object of learning mathematics is not pleasure, gain, or comfort. These things may result, but the true object is to give us a deeper understanding of God's character and law and prepare us to do *"good works"* (Epheisans 2:10).

A Garden

A Country Home

A Spiritual Educational Program

Reinforce

Find a Bible Verse for:

1. Place Value
2. Addition
3. Subtraction
4. Multiplication
5. Division

Use a *Strong's Concordance*

Write the
Bible references below.

1. _____

2. _____

3. _____

4. _____

5. _____

The Bible:
The Mathematics Book

The Bible lessons and illustrations become the focus of the Mathematics lesson rather than just learning "numbers." Each mathematics lesson should teach us something about God's character and the laws within which He works, and how we can apply them to our daily lives. Remember, He says, *"learn of me."*

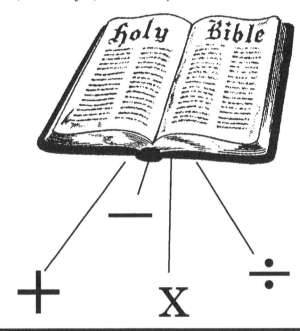

"Every man has in himself
a continent of undiscovered character.
Happy is he who acts the Columbus
to his own soul."
–Sir J. Stevens

Reinforce

1. Teacher, dictate the spelling words!
2. Do the Bible Mark on page 21.

The Lent Half-Dollar

Arthur helped when he saw a need.

"What are you crying for?" said Arthur to a little ragged boy that he overtook on his way home from the village school. There was something in the kind of crying that led Arthur to think that there was some serious cause for it.

"I'm hungry," said the boy, "and can't get nothing to eat."

"He don't go to our school, or he would have said 'can't get anything to eat.'" But Arthur did not stop to criticize his language.

"Why doesn't your Mother give you something to eat?"

"She hasn't anything for herself, and she is sick and can't get up."

"Where is your Father?"

"I haven't any. He was drowned at sea."

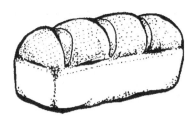

"Where do you live?"

"Down there" pointing to a miserable hut in the distance.

"Come with me and I will get you something." Arthur turned back and the boy followed him. He had a few cents in his pocket, just enough, as it proved, to buy a loaf of bread. He gave it to the boy and told him he would go home with him. The boy took the loaf, and though he did not break it, he looked at it so wishfully, that Arthur took his knife and cut off a piece and gave it to him to eat. He ate it in a manner that showed he had not deceived Arthur when he told him that he was hungry. The tears came into Arthur's eyes as he saw him swallow the dry bread with such eagerness. He remembered, with some self-reproach, that he had sometimes complained when he had nothing better than bread and butter for dinner. On their way to the boy's home, Arthur learned that the family had moved into the place about a week before and that his mother became sick the day after they came, and was unable to leave her bed—that there were children younger than himself—that their last food was eaten the day before—that his mother had sent him out to beg for the first time in his life—that the first man he asked, told him beggars would be put in jail; so he was afraid to ask anybody else, but was returning home when Arthur overtook him and asked him what he was crying for.

Arthur went in and saw a kind-looking woman on the bed with two small children crying by her side. As he opened the door, he heard the oldest say, "Do, Mama, give me something to eat." They stopped crying when Arthur and the boy came in. The boy ran to the bed and gave his mother the loaf, and pointing to Arthur, said, "He bought it for me."

"Thank you," said the woman, "may God bless you, and give you the bread of eternal life."

The oldest little girl jumped up and down in her joy, and the youngest tried to grab the loaf, and struggled hard to do so, but did not speak. Seeing that the widow's hands were weak, Arthur took the loaf and cut off a piece for the youngest first, and then for the girl and the boy. He then gave the loaf to the widow. She ate a small piece,

then closed her eyes, and seemed to be engaged in silent prayer.

"She must be one of the Lord's poor," thought Arthur. "I'll go and get something for you as soon as I can," said he, and left.

He went to Mrs. Burton, who lived near, and told her the story, and she immediately sent some milk, and bread, and butter, and sent word that she would come herself, as soon as she could get the baby to sleep.

Arthur had a half-dollar at home, which he wished to give to the poor woman. His father gave it to him for watching sheep, and told him he must not spend it, but put it out at interest, or trade with it so as to make something. He knew his father would not let him give it away, for he was not a Christian, and thought of little else than making and saving money. Arthur's mother had died when he was an infant. But with her last breath, she gave him to God.

When Arthur was five years old, he was sent to a school with a pious teacher, who cared for his soul; and knowing that he had no teacher at home, she took unusual pains to instruct him in the principles of religious truth. The Holy

Spirit helped her efforts, and before he was eight years of age, there was reason to hope that he had been converted.

Arthur was now in his tenth year. He considered how he should help the poor widow, and at last he hit upon the plan which proved successful.

His father wanted him to begin to act for himself in business matters, such as making bargains. He did not wish him to ask his advice in doing so, but to go by his own judgment. After the business was done, he would show him whether it was wise or not; but never criticized him, lest he should discourage him from acting on his own responsibility.

In view of these facts, Arthur formed his plan.

"Father, may I lend my half-dollar?"

"To some spendthrift boy?"

"I won't lend it without good security."

The father was pleased that his son had the idea of good security in his head; he would not ask what it was, for he wished Arthur to de-cide for himself. He told him to lend it, but be careful not to lose it.

"I'll be sure about that," said Arthur.

So he took the half-dollar, and ran to the poor widow, and gave it to her, and left before she had time to thank him.

At night, his father asked him if he had put out his money.

"Yes, sir."

"Who did you lend it to?"

"I gave it to a poor starving widow in Mr. Harvey's house."

There was a frown gathering on his father's brow as he said, "Do you call that lending? Did you not ask my permission to lend it? Have I a son that will deceive me?" "No, sir," said Arthur, "I did lend it." He opened his Bible, that he had ready, with his finger in the place, and read, "He that giveth to the poor, lendeth to the Lord." "I lent it to the Lord, Father, and I call that written promise good security."

"Lent it to the Lord! He will never pay you."

"Yes, He will; He says that He will repay again."

"I thought you had more sense," said his father, but this was not said in an angry tone. The truth was, the old man was pleased with the ingenuity, as he called it, of his son. He did not wish to discourage that. So he took out his purse and handed Arthur half a dollar. "Here, the Lord will never repay you; I must, or you will never see your money again."

"Thank you, sir," said Arthur.

"In my way of thinking, " said Arthur to himself, "the Lord has paid me, and much sooner than I expected, too; I didn't expect that He would pay me in money. The hearts of all men are in His hands, and the gold and silver are His; He has put it in my father's heart to pay it to me. I'll lend it again."

Arthur kept up the habit of lending his spare money to the Lord all his days, and he was always satisfied that he was paid back fourfold, and often several times over. God **loves** to see such kind-hearted boys and girls.

End

Reflect – Consider This:

A lighted piece of paper laid flat on a piece of metal will go out, for the metal absorbs the heat and starves the flame: so does gold laid close to the soul cause the holy flame of **love** to God to shrink and die. The heart cannot embrace God and money; and, therefore, if it give its affection and solicitude to the latter, it is guilty of idolatry. *"Mortify therefore your members which are upon the earth; fornication, uncleanness, inordinate affection, evil concupiscence, and covetousness, which is idolatry"* (Colossians 3:5).

+ Simple Arithmetic

If you add, my dear, to someone's joys,
Pray, tell me what you do.
Do not look puzzled, the answer is plain—
The joys are doubled for you!

—*Adelbert F. Caldwell*

=

♡"Greater Than This Hath No Man"

On one of the bridges of Ghent in Flanders are two bronze statues. They represent a father and son and are memorials of their mutual affection. On account of some grave political offence both were condemned to die by the headsman's axe. Such was the popular esteem in which they were held that an executioner could not be found. A strange proposition was made them, that one should have his life by becoming the executioner of the other. The proposal was hailed with a melancholy pleasure by both, because each saw how one life at least could be saved. The son urged the father to accept the terms as he could die happy, since in that way his father's life would be spared. The father urged the son to accept the terms. He spoke of his own life as soon to end at any rate, but the son had youth on his side and long life before him.

By earnest entreaties the father prevailed; the son consented. The day of execution came: a vast multitude had assembled to witness the strange sight. There was the horrid scaffold with its block and broad axe. Father and son are there, the one to be beheaded by the other. The father kneels, places his neck on the wood and awaits the fatal stroke which shall sever the grey head from the body. The son with pale face and wild look seizes the axe and lifts it with trembling hand. He strikes—No! he flings the deadly weapon from his hand and falls on the bare neck of his father bathing it with filial tears and examining, "No, no, my father, we die together!" The vast crowd whose feelings were strung to the highest pitch, gave vent to their admiration in the wildest applause and demanded their pardon, a demand which was not only granted, but which was followed up by the artist's genius in the rearing of a memorial of the noble act of mutual affection. *"Greater love hath no man than this, that a man lay down his life for his friends." "But God commendeth his love toward us, in that, while we were yet sinners* [enemies], *Christ died for us"* (John 15:13; Romans 5:8).

Reflect

A poor man in an asylum wrote these words upon a pane of glass in his cell:

Could we with ink the ocean fill,
  And were the skies of parchment made;
Was every stem on earth a quill,
  And every man a scribe by trade;
To write the **love** of God,
        would drain the ocean dry,
  Nor could the scroll contain the whole,
  Though stretched from sky to sky.

1. What does mathematics mean?

Matthew 11:29 – *"Learn of me; for I am meek and lowly in heart...."*

Note: Mathematics means "inclined to learn." Through it we will not only learn about addition, subtraction, multiplication, division, and other processes but we will receive a deeper understanding of the spiritual things of God as visualized through mathematics.

2. How did boy Jesus learn mathematics?

Mark 6:3 – *"Is not this the carpenter...?"*

Matthew 13:34-35 – *"All these things spake Jesus unto the multitude in parables; and without a parable spake he not unto them.*

"That it might be fulfilled which was spoken by the prophet, saying, I will open my mouth in parables; I will utter things which have been kept secret from the foundation of the world."

See Psalm 78:2.

Note: "He learned a trade, and with His own hands worked in the carpenter's shop with Joseph." *The Desire of Ages* 72 "...His intimate acquaintance with the Scriptures shows how diligently His early years were given to the study of God's word. And spread out before Him was the great library of God's created works." *The Desire of Ages* 70

And because of all this it is said:
Luke 2:40 – *"And the child grew, and waxed strong in spirit, filled with wisdom; and the grace of God was upon him."*

3. Mathematics in the carpenter shop included measuring, cutting, and building.

Revelation 11:1 – *"And there was given me a reed like unto a rod: and the angel stood, saying, Rise, and <u>measure</u> the temple of God, and the altar, and them that worship therein."*

I Peter 4:12 – *"Beloved, think it not strange concerning the <u>fiery trial</u> which is to try you, as though some strange thing happened unto you."*

Ephesians 2:21 – *"In whom all the <u>building</u> fitly framed together groweth unto an holy temple in the Lord."*

4. Mathematics can teach us about giving.

Luke 6:38 – *"Give, and it shall be given unto you; good measure, pressed down, and shaken together, and running over...."*

5. The Bible talks about measuring, the balance, numbers, weights, and many other things that relate to mathematics.

Isaiah 40:12 – *"Who hath <u>measured</u> the waters in the hollow of his hand, and meted out heaven with the <u>span</u>, and comprehended the dust of the earth in a <u>measure</u>, and <u>weighed</u> the mountains in scales, and the hills in a <u>balance</u>?"*

Psalm 147:4 – *"He telleth the <u>number</u> of the stars; he calleth them all by their names."*

Isaiah 40:26 – *"Lift up your eyes on high, and behold who hath created these things, that bringeth out their host by <u>number</u>: he calleth them all by names by the greatness of his might, for that he is strong in power; not one faileth."*

Job 28:25 – *"To make the <u>weight</u> for the winds; and he <u>weigheth</u> the waters by <u>measure</u>."*

Review
Place I - II - III

1. What is practical daily mathematics?

2. Explain the Greek way of learning mathematics and then the Hebrew way of learning mathematics.

3. Give examples from the Bible of mathematics.

4. Where is one good place to learn mathematics?

5. What is the object of learning mathematics?

6. Who designed mathematics?

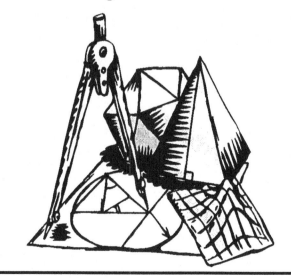

Outline of School Program

Age	Grade	Program
Birth through Age 7	Babies Kindergarten and Pre-school	*Family Bible Lessons* (This includes: Bible, Science–Nature, and Character)
Age 8	First Grade	*Family Bible Lessons* (This includes: Bible, Science–Nature, and Character) + Language Program (*Writing and Spelling Road to Reading and Thinking* [WSRRT])
Age 9-14 or 15	Second through Eighth Grade	*The Desire of all Nations* (This includes: Health, Mathematics, Music, Science–Nature, History/Geography/Prophecy, Language, and Voice–Speech) + Continue using WSRRT
Ages 15 or 16-19	Ninth through Twelfth Grade	9 – *Cross and Its Shadow I** + Appropriate Academic Books 10 – *Cross and Its Shadow II** + Appropriate Academic Books 11 – *Daniel the Prophet** + Appropriate Academic Books 12 – *The Seer of Patmos** (Revelation) + Appropriate Academic Books *or you could continue using *The Desire of Ages*
Ages 20-25	College	Apprenticeship

Made in the USA
Las Vegas, NV
26 September 2021